C0-DXD-908

358
W

Wright, Susan,

Weapons of mass destruction.
Illicit trade and trafficking
HOMESTEAD HS MEDIA CENTER
585928

DATE DUE			

THE LIBRARY OF WEAPONS OF MASS DESTRUCTION™

Weapons of Mass Destruction
Illicit Trade and Trafficking

SUSAN WRIGHT

The Rosen Publishing Group, Inc., New York

Published in 2005 by The Rosen Publishing Group, Inc.
29 East 21st Street, New York, NY 10010

Copyright © 2005 by The Rosen Publishing Group, Inc.

First Edition

All rights reserved. No part of this book may be reproduced in any form without permission in writing from the publisher, except by a reviewer.

Library of Congress Cataloging-in-Publication Data

Wright, Susan, 1939–
Weapons of mass destruction: illicit trade and trafficking / by Susan Wright.—1st ed.
   p. cm. —(The library of weapons of mass destruction)
Includes bibliographical references and index.
ISBN 1-4042-0297-8 (library binding)
1. Weapons of mass destruction—Juvenile literature. 2. Illegal arms transfers—Juvenile literature.
I. Title. II. Series.
U793.W75 2005
358'.3—dc22

2004010573

Manufactured in the United States of America

On the cover: Russian customs inspectors examine an incoming container for smuggled nuclear materials at a dock in Dudinka, Russia.

[CONTENTS]

INTRODUCTION 4

1 WHAT IS USED TO MAKE WEAPONS OF MASS DESTRUCTION? 8

2 WHERE DO THE MATERIALS FOR WMD COME FROM? 19

3 WHO IS SMUGGLING WMD? 32

4 WHAT ARE THE AUTHORITIES DOING ABOUT IT? 45

GLOSSARY 55
FOR MORE INFORMATION 57
FOR FURTHER READING 59
BIBLIOGRAPHY 60
INDEX 62

INTRODUCTION

What does an atomic engineer do when he or she can't make enough money to survive? One engineer in Russia became so disheartened when his pay was cut that he began to steal uranium. Leonid Smirnov was an employee at the Luch Scientific Production Association, a scientific manufacturing workshop in Russia. Over several months in 1992, Smirnov stole 3.5 pounds (1.6 kilograms) of uranium that was pure enough to be used in an atomic bomb.

Smirnov hid the uranium in a container on the balcony of his apartment. "I had no idea where to

Employees of the Russian Defense Ministry march in Moscow on October 31, 1996, to protest the government's failure to pay them for several months. Since the fall of the Soviet Union, many highly skilled workers, including those in the weapons industry, have lost their jobs, suffered a marked decline in salary and standard of living, or been forced to wait for extended periods to be paid for their work.

sell it," Smirnov said during an interview with PBS's *Frontline*. "I had no customers. I had no idea on the price. I just thought of appearing at foreign firms in Moscow to discuss the deal."

What drove Smirnov to try such a crazy scheme? Well, atomic scientists and engineers were in deep trouble after the Soviet Union dissolved in 1991. Separate countries were formed from the vast Communist empire—Russia, Ukraine, Belarus, Kazakhstan and Uzbekistan, to name a few. These countries were suddenly very poor when they emerged from under Soviet control and protection.

WEAPONS OF MASS DESTRUCTION: ILLICIT TRADE AND TRAFFICKING

The employees who worked for the atomic energy industry and in military facilities were once the elite of Soviet society. They enjoyed a higher standard of living than almost anyone else, earning approximately $190 a month in 1991. That was well above the national average wage of $128 a month. But in 1999, the average salary was just $43 a month. By then, many atomic experts were barely surviving on one-third the subsistence rate, the minimum amount of money needed to pay for food, clothing, and shelter.

Russian atomic industry workers picketed the Ministry of Finance in Moscow, Russia, in October 1996. Two months later, more than a dozen employees at the St. Petersburg nuclear power plant, which generates most of the city's electrical power, took over the plant's control room. They threatened to close down the plant unless they were paid months of back wages. The Russian government immediately flew in more than 1 billion rubles ($37 million) to prevent a crisis.

These highly qualified specialists were earning less than the cleaning women who worked in the Moscow subway. Many were forced to take second jobs and sell vegetables from their own gardens in order to make ends meet. These were the people with atomic bombs in their hands.

Disgruntled employees are just one source for the atomic, chemical, and biological materials that are brought into the weapons black market. A black market is a trade network for illegal goods. People are usually motivated by money when they steal or smuggle dangerous materials. But terrorists who buy, manufacture,

Leonid Smirnov was a foreman at a Russian uranium waste site when he stole the highly enriched uranium. He got the idea after reading an article on nuclear theft in a local newspaper. No one noticed that the uranium was missing until after Smirnov was caught.

and use these terrifying weapons are often trying to further their fanatic religious or nationalist beliefs.

When money, fanaticism, and weapons of mass destruction (WMD) come together, they make a very dangerous combination. WMD are capable of inflicting large numbers of casualties and widespread property damage. This book will explore where weapons of mass destruction come from, how they fall into the wrong hands, and what nations around the world are doing to combat this illicit trade.

If you're wondering what happened to Leonid Smirnov, the engineer who stole the uranium, he was arrested while boarding a train to Moscow, where he planned to search for a buyer. A Russian court sentenced Smirnov to only three years probation. It wasn't until 2002, ten years later, that Russia began imposing stricter punishments for stealing and smuggling material that can be used to make weapons of mass destruction.

1

WHAT IS USED TO MAKE WEAPONS OF MASS DESTRUCTION?

Weapons of mass destruction are different from conventional weapons such as guns or bombs because of the enormous damage they can wreak on people and cities. There are growing concerns that terrorists will use WMD instead of conventional weapons and kidnappings to inflict terror. The U.S. government takes this threat seriously since terrorist activities in the United States have increased in the past decade, most notably with the September 11, 2001, attacks on the World Trade Center and the Pentagon.

A large part of the concern stems from the reality that many stockpiles of atomic, chemical, and biological materials aren't protected by effective security measures. This creates opportunities for rogue nations and terrorist groups to acquire material that can be used to make WMD. There are also fears that scientists from the former Soviet Union and other countries will sell their expertise to help terrorists build WMD.

DANGEROUS MATERIALS

Weapons of mass destruction can be separated into three categories: atomic, chemical, and biological weapons. Each of these dangerous materials involves special concerns when it comes to preventing illicit trade and trafficking.

ATOMIC WEAPONS

For four decades during the Cold War, everyone feared the possibility of an atomic attack by either the United States or the former Soviet Union. The two superpowers were locked in an arms race that built up huge stockpiles of nuclear warheads (atomic bombs carried by missiles), each capable of killing 100,000 people. One Russian intercontinental ballistic missile (ICBM) is five times more powerful than the total number of conventional bombs the United States dropped on Iraq during the entire Gulf War in 1991.

During the Cold War, the Soviet Union and the United States created industries with numerous facilities that employed atomic material. Because of poor accounting systems and inadequate security, it is impossible to know how many pounds of atomic material are currently unaccounted for, especially in the nations of the former Soviet Union.

Russian nuclear workers prepare to replace a nuclear missile on a launchpad in Russia's Saratov region on May 14, 2002. Russia possesses approximately 20,000 nuclear weapons and large quantities of other nuclear materials.

This material is smuggled from country to country. Fifteen pounds (6.8 kg) of plutonium or 30 pounds (13.6 kg) of uranium is needed for an atomic weapon. Once there is enough atomic material, it takes about $100,000 to create a bomb. Oil-rich countries are watched carefully because they have the funds to make such a weapon.

A much easier weapon for terrorists to construct is a so-called dirty bomb created from conventional explosives and a small amount of atomic material. To make a dirty bomb, it is not necessary to use plutonium or uranium. Atomic materials such as cesium 137, strontium 90, and cobalt 60 are widely available for industrial and research purposes.

Dirty bombs fling atomic material into the fallout caused by the bomb's explosion. They carry a lot of punch for their small size. This type of threat was first used in 1995, when Chechen rebels placed a lead container with cesium 137 in Moscow's Izmailovo Park. The bomb was fortunately retrieved without being detonated.

In 2002, Chechen rebels were again suspected of stealing material from a Russian atomic power station. U.S. officials feared that the Chechens would supply this material to Iraq or Libya so that they might make atomic bombs.

CHEMICAL WEAPONS

Chemical weapons are preferred by terrorists because they are easier than atomic weapons to make and deliver. A chemical weapon is a toxin that kills or injures people by affecting the lungs, blood, eyes, nerves, and other organs. A person or animal must come into direct contact with enough of the chemical to be affected.

Chemical weapons can be divided into four classes: choking agents such as chlorine, blood agents such as hydrogen cyanide, nerve agents such as sarin, and blister agents such as mustard gas.

A chemical weapon could be as simple as a 50-gallon (189.3 liters) drum of chlorine. If explosives are used to blow up the drum, the poisonous plume could affect hundreds of people downwind. Chlorine gas was originally used on a massive scale by Germany in the second battle of Ypres in 1915 during World War I. Five thousand Allied soldiers were

> German soldiers release chlorine gas downwind toward French and Algerian troops in Ypres, Belgium, in 1915 during World War I. It was the first use of a chemical agent as a weapon of mass destruction.

killed and many more were injured in this chemical attack.

More than twenty nations now have the ability to produce chemical weapons. The former Soviet Union was the world's main manufacturer of deadly chemicals. After the breakup of that country, Russia alone possessed 40,000 tons of chemical weapons.

Each chemical must be delivered in a specific way. Technical information describing which delivery system works best for each chemical is available readily on the Internet. For example, hydrogen cyanide vaporizes quickly and has limited outdoor use, whereas mustard gas can hang in the air and thus contaminate a large outdoor area. Some gases must be delivered using explosives or sprayers. Others can be poured out.

In the 1993 World Trade Center bombing, the terrorists not only attempted to topple the north tower into the south tower, but they also included sodium cyanide in the explosives. Fortunately, the chemicals burned when the bomb was detonated rather than being vaporized and sucked up into the north tower to kill everyone inside.

BIOLOGICAL WEAPONS

Biological weapons are easy to produce and difficult to detect. These weapons are used in what is called germ warfare because any infectious agent such as a bacterium or virus can be used to inflict harm on people, livestock, or crops. Biological agents include living microorganisms such as bacteria, viruses, and fungi, as well as toxins (chemicals) produced by microorganisms, plants, or animals. Bacterial agents are more likely to be used as weapons because they are easier to cultivate and less perishable than viruses.

Biological weapons are very different from chemical or atomic weapons because they do not cause dramatic explosions. The effects of a biological attack appear slowly after an incubation period. Laboratory testing is required to single out a biological attack from something ordinary like the flu or stomach poisoning. A biological agent could become more lethal if it is contagious, unless it can be countered with an antidote.

On a pound-for-pound basis, biological agents are much more deadly than chemical weapons. In the right environment they can multiply at a rapid rate. They can also naturally mutate, preventing antidotes from working. Even a tiny amount of a disease organism can be used as a weapon.

The history of biological warfare goes back much further than the use of chemicals. The bubonic plague of the fourteenth century, which killed nearly one-third of the population of Europe, was allegedly spread by the Tartars besieging the fortress of Caffa in the Crimea, in present-day Ukraine. The Tartars catapulted plague-infected corpses into the fortress. Ships are said to have carried the disease to northern Italy and the rest of Europe.

Japan followed the Tartars' lead by dropping plague-infested fleas and grain from airplanes over Chinese cities after its 1937 invasion of China. A special biological warfare unit called 731 was created under General Ishi in Manchuria that produced many biological agents, including the plague, smallpox, typhus, and

[Russian workers dressed in full protective suits perform a routine check of barrels of toxic agents at a chemical weapons storage site in Gorny, Russia, on May 20, 2000. With financial assistance from the United States and other western nations, Russia has begun destroying its stockpile of chemical weapons.]

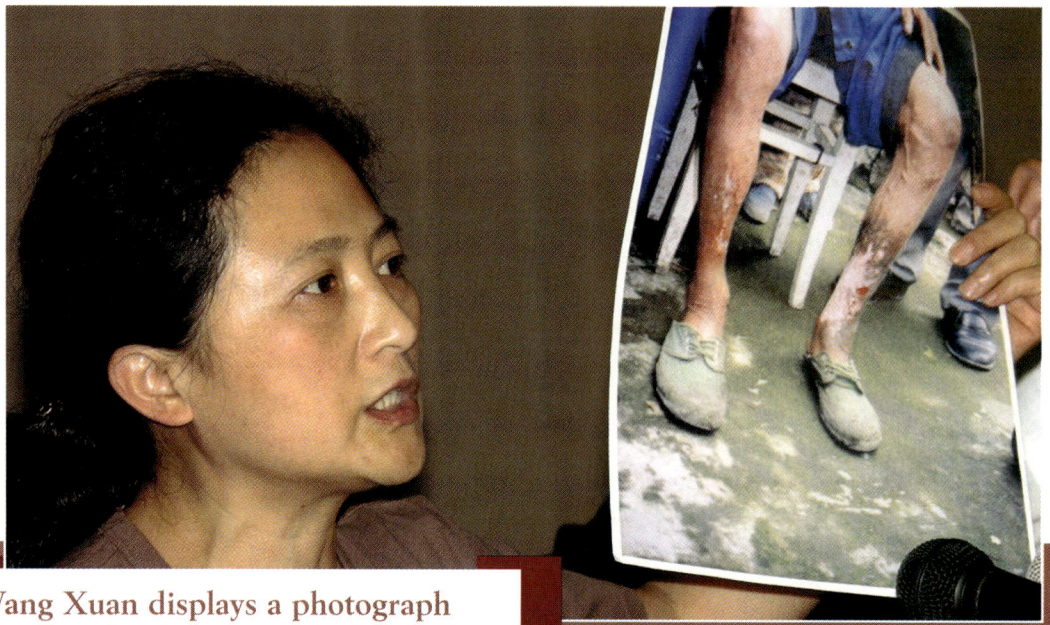

Wang Xuan displays a photograph showing the damage to the legs of a Chinese citizen on whom the Japanese Imperial Army allegedly performed biological weapons experiments during World War II. She represented 180 Chinese victims who unsuccessfully sued the Japanese government for the atrocity in 2002.

gas gangrene. Ten thousand people were killed when tests were performed on Chinese civilians and prisoners of war.

Currently, at least fourteen countries have the ability to engage in biological weapons programs or already have stockpiles of material.

TECHNOLOGY TO MAKE WMD

A trade network for WMD materials has sprung up since the end of the Cold War that extends through Europe, Asia, and the countries of the former Soviet Union. Also, pieces of equipment to make WMD can be bought from many different suppliers. For example, an atomic weapon requires 4,000 components for power, arming, triggering the device, and synchronizing the interactive parts. Most of the components are used in ordinary equipment: springs, spacers, connectors, switches, relays, condensers, wiring, and computer and electrical systems.

Technical information on how to make WMD is readily available on the Internet, along with tips on acquiring plutonium. Terrorists can easily find a step-by-step guide on how to create atomic bombs in a non-laboratory

WHAT IS USED TO MAKE WEAPONS OF MASS DESTRUCTION?

setting. For example, a sphere of compacted plutonium oxide crystals can be placed inside a large cube of Semtex or some other kind of explosive. The finished bomb weighs approximately one ton and can be delivered either by van or missile.

For biological weapons, almost all of the laboratory equipment used to cultivate microorganisms has legitimate uses in the production of beer, wine, food, animal feed, vaccines, and pharmaceuticals. This

SARIN ATTACK IN JAPAN

Aerial view of Aum Shinrikyo's facilities in Kamikuishiki Village, at the foot of Mount Fuji

The most infamous chemical attack took place on the morning of March 20, 1995, in Japan. A religious cult called Aum Shinrikyo (Supreme Truth) placed containers of sarin nerve gas on five trains of the Tokyo subway. The chemical killed twelve people and injured 5,500 more. There were a relatively low number of deaths because of Aum Shinrikyo's crude delivery method—they used eleven plastic bags with holes punched in them.

Aum Shinrikyo was not a secret organization; members regularly paraded around Tokyo wearing masks of the face of their guru and leader, Asahara Shoko. The cult had acquired tons of dangerous chemicals that were stored in warehouses close to the Aum Shinrikyo training center near Mount Fuji. Only nine members of the cult were convicted of murder, attempted murder, and lesser charges for the attack.

In January 1999, the United States imposed economic sanctions against the Moscow Aviation Institute *(pictured here)* and two other Russian institutions for allegedly failing to prevent leaks of nuclear and missile technology to Iran.

technology is also available on the Internet for anyone to access, while academic conferences provide information on the latest innovations.

Chemical weapons are even easier to make with equipment and material used to manufacture pesticides, insecticides, household cleaners, drugs, and other compounds.

WMD EXPERTS

Making a chemical or biological weapon doesn't require as much technical knowledge as making an atomic weapon. A second- or third-year biology student could create the growth medium for bacteria or viruses.

However, to construct a lethal weapon, terrorists also need to know about the development of diseases, drug interactions and the physics involved in delivery methods. As the Aum Shinrikyo discovered in Japan, you have to know how to distribute the deadly material in order to make an effective weapon.

The chemical and biological materials are just as dangerous for the terrorists as for their intended victims. Safety procedures must be established by experts and include a well-designed laboratory and protective clothing. Experts also must be brought in to design, assemble, and test the weapons.

Unfortunately, the number of qualified experts with skills and experience is growing. More than 60,000 weapons scientists and technicians were once part of the formidable Soviet weapons and aerospace programs. In Russia alone, there were more than 20,000 atomic and missile specialists whose knowledge could be used to help terrorists.

Many Soviet experts found a haven in Iran, which has sponsored an atomic weapons program since the early 1990s. Vadim Vorobei, head of engine production at the Moscow Aviation Institute, was paid to go to Tehran, Iran, starting in 1996, to give lectures on rocket technology to Iranian university students. Vorobei agreed because after the Soviet Union fell, he no longer had the privileges he was used to. These included paid vacations, a heavily subsidized apartment, access to special stores, free medical care and a dacha (a house in the country). Almost overnight,

WEAPONS OF MASS DESTRUCTION: ILLICIT TRADE AND TRAFFICKING

Vorobei, Leonid Smirnov, and thousands of other highly trained experts were destitute.

For five years, Vorobei kept running into foreign specialists and engineers who were also willing to sell their services. Yet Iran's weapons program moved slowly. "They created an engine, but not a proper guidance system," Vorobei said, as quoted in a January 13, 2002, *Washington Post* article by Michael Dobbs. "They don't have any real metallurgical industry of their own. Their only hope is to steal something from neighboring countries, but they can't steal everything."

> *"Their only hope is to steal something from neighboring countries, but they can't steal everything."*
>
> ***Vadim Vorobei***

The United States has also trained scientists who have assisted foreign WMD programs. The work on the Libyan atomic weapons program was done in part by Libyan scientists who had studied at the Universities of Wisconsin and Minnesota, as well as at the University of Exeter in Great Britain. China took full advantage of science and engineering training available in the United States. Future leaders of China's atomic and missile programs were enrolled in U.S. universities as early as the 1950s, and by the 1980s, tens of thousands of state-sponsored Chinese students were in the United States. The training and education has long been available for anyone to access.

> Russia's Shikhany Research Center is one of the world's most important sites for researching chemical and biological weapons. It has been in operation since 1926, when it was established under a secret agreement between the Soviet Union and Germany.

WHERE DO THE MATERIALS FOR WMD COME FROM?

Many of the materials that can be used to make atomic, chemical, or biological weapons have legitimate uses in medical laboratories, energy production, pest control, and research, just to name a few. These materials are referred to as dual-use materials.

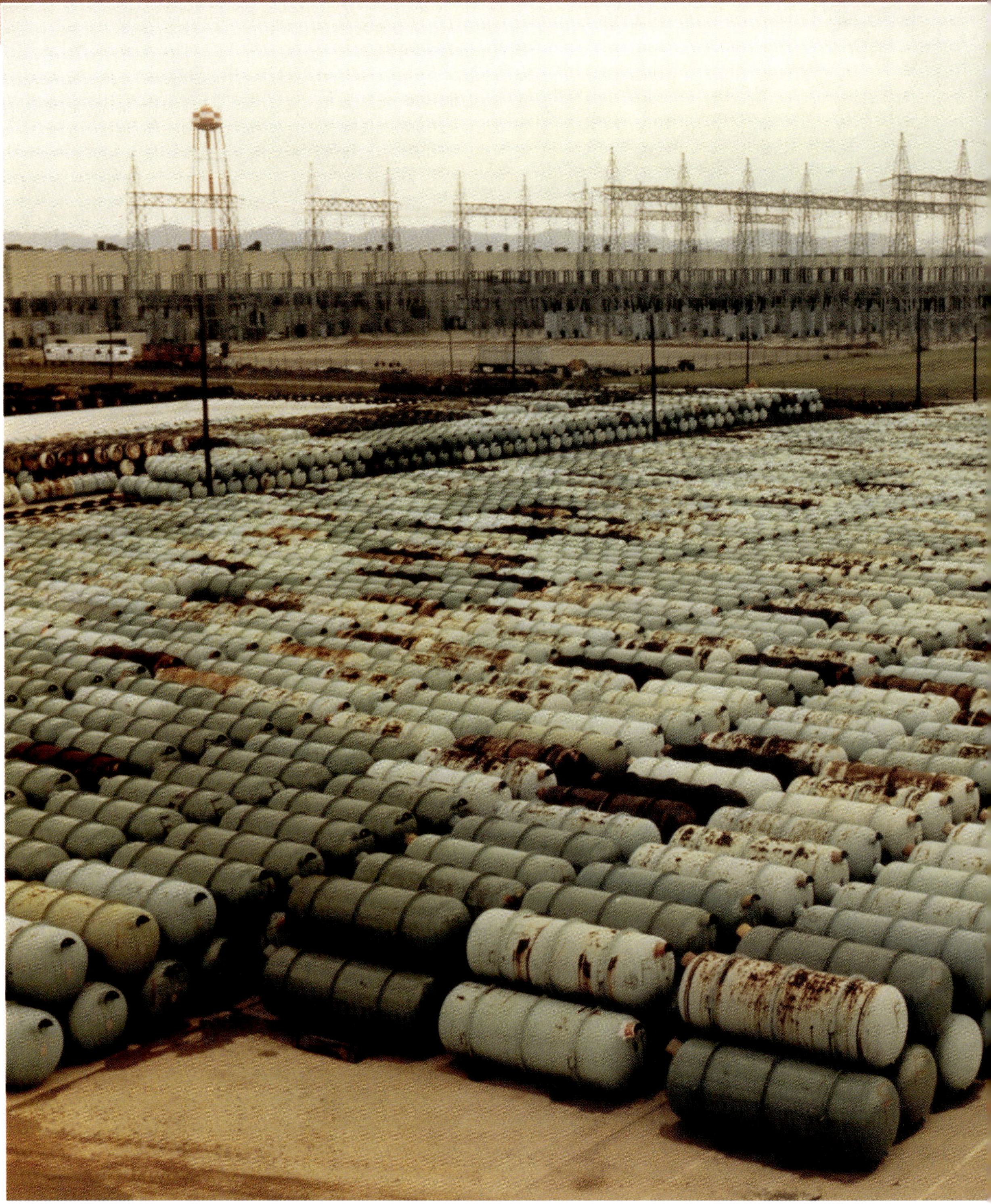

It is difficult to protect dual-use materials from falling into the hands of terrorists while not interfering with legitimate trade. There are currently 65,000 chemicals alone on the dual-use list. There are a number of international laws to control the manufacture and use of these dangerous chemicals, but some nations freely trade them to rogue nations and groups with questionable intentions.

ORIGINAL USES

Many chemicals that are used in pharmaceuticals, plasticizers, and cleaning agents are considered dual-use materials. A number of industries have such large stockpiles that sizable amounts could be stolen without detection. Truckloads of chemicals used in herbicides, insecticides, or rodenticides are on the roads every day, making them vulnerable to hijacking and theft.

Isopropyl alcohol, which terrorists can use to manufacture chemical poisons, is also available in large quantities. Arsenic and strychnine were

[Thousands of fourteen-ton storage cylinders line this uranium tails yard at a nuclear fuel production facility in Ohio. Uranium tails are U-238 isotopes removed during the nuclear enrichment process. Each cylinder has the energy potential of 2.5 billion gallons (9.5 billion L) of oil.]

once regularly used for medical purposes. Eserin, one of the first nerve gases, was originally used in a drug for glaucoma. Ricin can be extracted from ordinary castor beans.

For biological weapons, it all starts with a germ or virus. Many of these microorganisms can be obtained directly from nature, such as anthrax from sheep, staphylococcus from chickens, and Lassa fever from wild rodents in West Africa. To obtain samples, an expert is needed to identify, analyze, and extract the desired material. It is much easier to steal the biological material from medical and research laboratories, or to simply purchase it for a few dollars from the businesses that supply the labs, than it is to extract it from natural sources.

Atomic materials are used in numerous agricultural, research, medical, and energy production purposes. Tiny amounts of atomic material power smoke alarms, remote beacons, and exit signs. Many industrial gauges are run by atomic material. Gamma radiation from cesium 137 and cobalt 60 are used to calibrate instruments and to measure the thickness and density of industrial materials. There is also natural uranium, which can be found in ore and powder form.

In the medical field alone, 100 types of atomic material are used in research, diagnosis, and treatment. Patients have benefited from medical equipment that is sterilized by atomic technology. Millions of cancer patients have had their lives prolonged by radiation treatments.

Of greatest concern is atomic material that has been enriched, which increases its power. More than 130 research reactors around the world still use enriched uranium, yet many have no more security than a night watchman and a chain-link fence. More than fifty countries have atomic waste waiting for disposal in temporary sites with questionable security.

Nuclear warheads also use enriched atomic material. As of January 2003, the United States still had 5,948 nuclear warheads, while Russia had 4,852 warheads (down from approximately 11,000 each in 1999). Under the 2002 Treaty on Strategic Offensive Reductions (SORT), these warheads will be reduced to between 1,700 and 2,200. However, the treaty allows both countries to store the warheads rather than dispose of the atomic material, which increases the

These ships, photographed in Murmansk, Russia, are used for storing nuclear waste. Nuclear waste can remain radioactive for tens of thousands of years, so ships like these provide only a temporary solution for the disposal of nuclear waste.

risk of theft of the atomic material.

In Russia, about 1,200 metric tons of enriched atomic material that can be used to make weapons are stored at more than fifty sites. This material is in research facilities, educational institutes, weapons assembly plants, nuclear reactor sites, transportation depots, warehouses, and storage yards. Defense-related sites that have atomic material include naval shipyards, fueling stations, chemical combines, uranium and plutonium separation plants, atomic weapons research institutes, and nuclear submarines.

An estimated 400 tons of atomic material in former Soviet facilities are considered to be at risk of theft because of poor security. A study by the Institute for International Studies at Stanford University in 2002 found that over the past ten years, at least 88 pounds (40 kg) of weapons-usable plutonium has been stolen from these poorly protected nuclear facilities. While most of it has been retrieved, at least 4.4 pounds (2 kg) of highly enriched uranium stolen from a nuclear reactor complex in the Republic of Georgia remains missing.

In 1996, the Monterey Center for Non-Proliferation Studies sent an observer to the National Nuclear Research Center in Kazakhstan. He reported that the electricity was disconnected in parts of the compound to save money and the facility that stored uranium was crumbling.

There are also a number of civilian-run facilities for physics, power engineering, research, and design of atomic reactors. Cesium was stolen from the Guryev oil refinery in Kazakhstan and the Fosforit chemical association in St. Petersburg, as well as from an asphalt-cement complex in Kaliningrad. At the Tomsk Institute of Nuclear Physics at the Polytechnical University, one fuel rod with enriched uranium disappeared and was never recovered.

At the handful of Russian sites where hundreds of tons of chemical agents are stored, the security is also sadly lacking: no tamper-proof locks, closed-circuit TV, or alarm systems that monitor motion and sound. It wasn't until 1996 that Russia officially recognized the problem of dangerous materials being stolen and smuggled from the country.

NATIONS THAT TRADE WMD

Unfortunately, many of the components for making WMD can be purchased as well as stolen and smuggled. All it requires is an export license to transport dual-use materials and equipment.

For example, businesses weren't allowed to sell powerful supercomputers to Chinese companies without an export license until 2002. But that didn't stop China from acquiring more than 1,000 supercomputers, like those being used by the U.S. National Security Agency and Los Alamos National Laboratories to design atomic weapons.

Businesses in the United States, Europe, and Asia continue to sell materials, expertise, and technology that can be used to make WMD. Nations that are developing illicit weapons programs can legally buy machine tools, spare parts for dual-use equipment, missile-related information, training, scientific equipment, and specialty metals.

Government-run weapons programs are the most serious threat because some nations are willing to make money from the weapons they've developed. Currently, Russia and China are the two main suppliers of WMD-related goods and training.

WHERE DO THE MATERIALS FOR WMD COME FROM?

RUSSIA

Russian firms belonging to the Russian Ministry of Atomic Energy are free to export weapons-grade materials including plutonium and cesium 137. For other Russian companies, export licenses can be obtained through organized crime syndicates or corrupt officials. Exporters can also misrepresent what they are trading in the customs forms.

The state-run defense and atomic industries are encouraged to produce exports for foreign trade. Some Russian universities and scientific institutes also earn money by providing chemical, biological, or missile-related training for foreign students.

LOOSE NUKES

General Aleksandr Lebed, a national security adviser during the government of Russian president Boris Yeltsin, claimed that the Soviet military industry had produced 250 "luggage nukes" in the 1970s. He described them as small atomic bombs built like suitcases that one person can carry. Lebed claimed in interviews in 1997 that 100 of the suitcase nukes were missing. However, U.S. and Russian officials publicly questioned Lebed's assertion, and are skeptical that suitcase nukes even exist.

Alexei Yablokov, a former Yeltsin adviser on environmental protection and a member of the Russian Academy of Sciences, confirmed that a "suitcase variant" of atomic weapons had been built to order by the KGB, the Soviet secret service. The United States also created hundreds of portable atomic bombs in the 1960s. The same year General Lebed dropped his bombshell, a film entitled *The Peacemaker* featured the theft of a Russian atomic bomb that could be carried in a backpack. In the film, the device was stolen as it was being transported by train across barren Siberia.

General Aleksandr Lebed

Russians have supplied goods and technology for WMD to Iran, China, Pakistan, Libya, and India. In 2002, Iranian scientists were being taught at the Nikiet Nuclear Research Institute outside of Moscow. In 2003, Russia helped construct the Bushehr Nuclear Power Plant project in Iran. Russia supplied material for India's atomic power plants and also sold them two atomic power reactors.

CHINA

China worked closely with the Soviet Union on its atomic weapons program, and more recently, Russia sold China nuclear accelerators worth more than $5 million. Russia also supplied China with missile components, ring magnets for computer memory cores, and a special industrial furnace that could be used to mold uranium into a bomb.

China has been regularly criticized by the United States and other countries for selling atomic equipment to Pakistan, Iran, North Korea, and Libya. Firms in China have also provided technical assistance to Pakistan to produce missiles to carry WMD.

China is working on two atomic projects in Iran—a small research reactor and a zirconium production facility. In 1997, China pledged to quickly bring these projects to an end, stating that it would not continue its new cooperation with Iran. However, Chinese businesses continue to supply weapons equipment and technology to Iran. Since 1997, the United States has repeatedly imposed sanctions against companies and individuals in China for trading dangerous materials, products, and missile components.

In November 2000, China made an agreement with the United States that it would stop exporting missiles and missile technology to other nations in exchange for U.S. licenses for commercial space programs. However, in early 2002, China insisted that it had not agreed to halt the WMD programs it already had under way.

HOW ARE WMD SMUGGLED?

There is a worldwide smuggling network that connects every part of the world. Drugs, weapons, and illegal goods are traded on this black

WHERE DO THE MATERIALS FOR WMD COME FROM?

This is the main building of Iran's Bushehr nuclear power plant, where the International Atomic Energy Agency (IAEA) and the United States suspect that Iran may be running a secret nuclear weapons program. The IAEA found traces of highly enriched, weapons-grade uranium at Bushehr in 2003. The inset photo shows Russian-made equipment used at the plant.

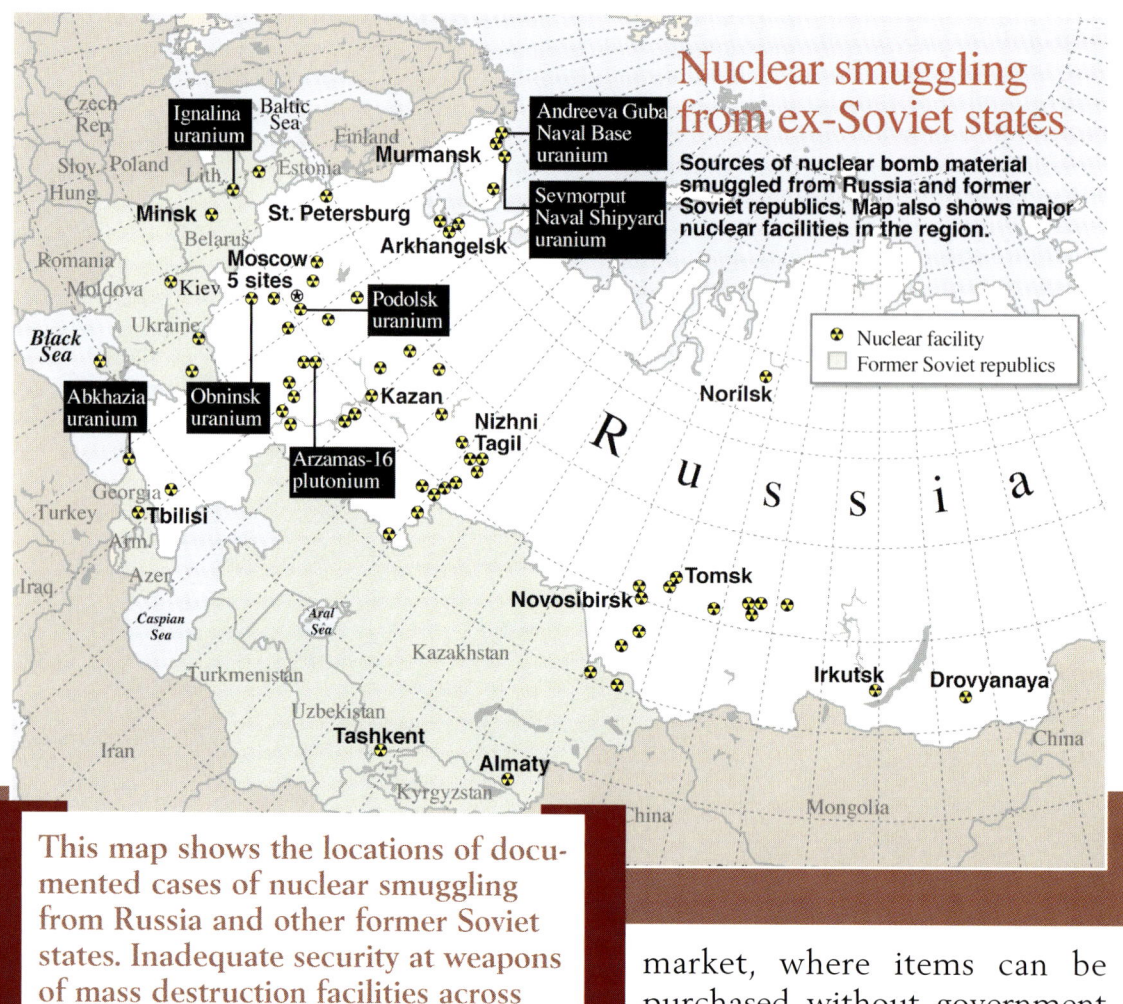

Nuclear smuggling from ex-Soviet states

Sources of nuclear bomb material smuggled from Russia and former Soviet republics. Map also shows major nuclear facilities in the region.

☢ Nuclear facility
▢ Former Soviet republics

This map shows the locations of documented cases of nuclear smuggling from Russia and other former Soviet states. Inadequate security at weapons of mass destruction facilities across the former Soviet Union increases the risk of terrorists acquiring these dangerous materials.

market, where items can be purchased without government or regulatory oversight.

Countries that are smuggler-friendly are likely to have shaky economies, rampant crime, and poorly paid customs officials and law enforcement officers. These countries offer well-established routes for transporting illicit materials.

The police and customs bureaus are well established in Europe and are capable of intercepting dangerous materials. The International Criminal Police Organization (Interpol) and the International Atomic Energy Agency (IAEA) have tracked the main flow of atomic material from Russia, through Belarus or the Baltic states, into central Europe.

However, it is likely that unrecorded incidents of smuggling are taking direct routes out of the former Soviet Union into the Middle East and Asia. It is possible to travel without detection through the deserts, over the mountains, and along the coastline via the Black Sea and Caspian ports. From there, the materials and equipment could be moved overland across central Asia.

In particular, the region between the Black and Caspian Seas has long been a key area for smuggling. Vladimir Orlov, editor of the Russian journal *Nuclear Control*, addressed the smuggling in this region in an essay entitled "Export Controls and Nuclear Smuggling in Russia." He wrote, "Anyone interested in smuggling issues should pay attention to Nazran International Airport. Though a small town, Nazran is the capital of Republic of Ingushetia, which is part of Russia but has no declared border with its neighbor Chechnya. Nazran has official duty-free status and is a center of criminal activities in the region. From Nazran International, there are regular and charter flights to Turkey, Greece, and other states of the Mediterranean and the Middle East. At the airport checkpoints, there is practically no control over goods transferred."

> "Nazran has official duty-free status and is a center of criminal activities in the region . . . At the airport checkpoints, there is practically no control over goods transferred."
>
> *Vladmir Orlov*

CUSTOMS

Customs agencies exist in almost every nation to prevent the importing and exporting of illegal goods. Customs officials are authorized to search trade goods, packages, and luggage without a warrant.

Materials that can be used to make WMD have been hidden in cargo containers, suitcase compartments, aerosol containers, and soles of shoes. Fully assembled atomic weapons can be delivered in the hold of a ship or an airplane. After the 9/11 attacks, U.S. and Norwegian intelligence agencies announced that they were trying to track down twenty-three

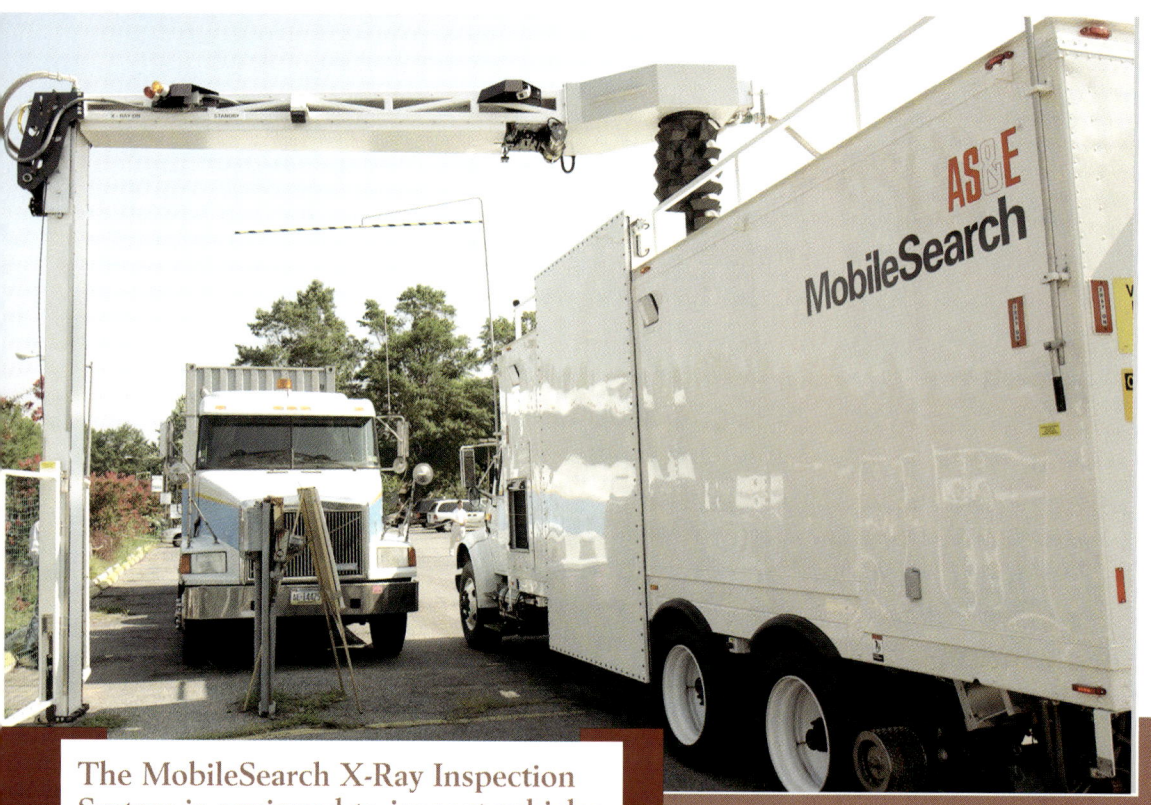

The MobileSearch X-Ray Inspection System is equipped to inspect vehicles and cargo for even small amounts of radioactive material, which could be used in a dirty bomb. U.S. Customs and Border Patrol also deploys MobileSearch along the U.S.-Mexican border to detect drugs, bomb-making materials, and illegal aliens.

merchant ships that were owned or controlled by the Al Qaeda terrorist network.

One reason Russia is a prime source of weapons material is because of its poor customs control along the borders. By late 2002, only 60 percent of the 300 customs posts along Russia's 40,000-mile (64,374 kilometers) border had working radiation monitors. Most of this equipment cannot distinguish between one type of radioactive metal from another, so smugglers can mislabel plutonium or uranium as legal cargo. Gamma spectrometers are able to scan the containers and detect specific atomic materials, but Russia lacks the funds to buy this equipment.

The U.S. Customs Service, with Department of Energy support, trains foreign customs officers to identify atomic materials, equipment, and technology. By late 1996, X-ray vans were deployed in Belarus, the Ukraine and the Baltic states. The United States gave Kazakhstan 100 handheld radiation detectors and $700,000 worth of laboratory equipment for analyzing atomic material samples.

U.S. Customs also teaches foreign customs agents to use portal range finders to locate false walls and concealed compartments in storage containers. Fiber-optic scopes can peer inside gas tanks and other enclosed spaces. Steel probes can detect material hidden inside bulk goods. And, with noses that are 10,000 times more sensitive than ours, dogs are used at airports to sniff out explosives, drugs, and chemical agents.

Controlling the transport of materials that can be used to make WMD is very difficult. But customs officials are at work around the world to prevent the trade and trafficking of dangerous materials. ■

3 WHO IS SMUGGLING WMD?

The Russian customs agency documented more than 500 attempts to smuggle atomic materials that were not weapons-grade across Russia's national frontiers in 2000. However only one case was reported to the IAEA. There were also at least 375 incidents of non-weapons-grade atomic materials or equipment that have been lost or stolen.

However, Russia claims that the number of smuggling attempts in Russia has dropped since the mid-1990s because of increased security. Western police agencies have documented eighteen cases in the past decade where weapons-grade uranium was stolen from Russia. In one notable example, Captain Alexei Tikhomirov sneaked through a hole in the fence at the Sevmorput naval shipyard in Murmansk, Russia, and took 10 pounds (4.5 kg) of enriched uranium from a fuel rod stored in a shed. Tikhomirov and his accomplices were arrested in 1994, when they tried to sell the stolen uranium.

Worldwide, there was a total of eight incidents of smuggling enriched atomic material between 2000 and 2002. The arrests took place in Europe and the countries of the former Soviet Union. Smugglers intended to provide material to terrorist groups, organized crime, and nations that are covertly sponsoring programs to produce weapons of mass destruction.

TERRORIST GROUPS

Terrorists engage in violence against political establishments, certain sections of society, or random individuals within a targeted state. Terrorists usually consider themselves freedom fighters for political, social, religious, or economic justice. Moderate movements that use nonviolent methods of protest to end oppression or spark social revolution are sometimes associated with radical fringe groups that use violence to gain their goals.

Lone individuals who are fanatics or psychopaths can also become terrorists. Fanatics have a fervent belief in a certain ideology, while psychopaths have a disregard toward others and refuse to follow normal rules of behavior. Judging from recent trends in terrorist attacks, fanaticism has become a driving force in international terrorism.

Among the thirty-three identified foreign terrorist organizations, many have expressed an interest in acquiring weapons of mass destruction. The arrest of terrorists planning to use ricin in London in January 2003, suggests that terrorist plots to use WMD may be more

This welder assembles a machine at a major Russian producer of fuel elements and assemblies used in nuclear power plants. Disgruntled by low wages, some Russian workers with access to weapons materials have resorted to smuggling to supplement their incomes.

British counterterrorism police investigators remove documents and a computer from the Finsbury Park Mosque in London, England, on January 20, 2003. The police raided the mosque and arrested seven people there as part of an investigation into the discovery of ricin in a London apartment two weeks earlier.

advanced than previously thought. Terrorist groups could also launch conventional attacks against chemical or atomic facilities to cause panic and economic disruption.

As early as 1998, Al Qaeda leader Osama bin Laden publicly declared that acquiring weapons of mass destruction is "a religious duty." A senior bin Laden associate on trial in Egypt in 1999 claimed that his group already had chemical and biological weapons. Individuals from terrorist groups worldwide received poison training at Al Qaeda–sponsored camps in Afghanistan. Al Qaeda also tried to buy enriched uranium in Sudan in the early 1990s, according to a U.S. government witness at the trial of the bombing of the U.S. embassies in Kenya and Tanzania in 1998.

WMD have already been used to attack people in the United States. Deadly anthrax was mailed to senators and media targets after September 11, 2001, killing five people and highlighting the vulnerability of civilian and government employees. However, the Federal Bureau of Investigation believes that an American scientist who has no known association with a terrorist organization was behind the attacks. Further, in 2002, a former gang member who was a convert to Islam was arrested in Chicago in connection with an Al Qaeda plot to detonate a dirty bomb. Experts warn there is a risk of another attack within the United States, possibly using WMD.

MOONLIGHTING AS SMUGGLERS

The most unlikely people have been caught smuggling atomic materials. Professional metals traders in Russia have sold atomic materials on the side. Scientists in need of cash have supported the smuggling network by providing certification services for stolen atomic material. Government employees such as trade officials, intelligence agents, and diplomats have assisted in atomic smuggling. In one bizarre case, Italian deputy prosecutor Romano Dolce, who spent years combating atomic smuggling between Switzerland and Italy, was arrested in 1993 and convicted for illegal nuclear trade. Ironically, Dolce had been one of the first to raise the alarm about atomic thefts from the former Soviet Union.

A firefighter and an FBI agent clean themselves up on October 9, 2001, after exiting the American Media building in Boca Raton, Florida, which tested positive for anthrax. The anthrax used in the attack came from U.S. military supplies, prompting concerns about the security of American inventories of this hazardous agent.

ORGANIZED CRIME

Organized crime syndicates have well-established smuggling routes for drugs and other illegal goods that they can use to transport WMD. A smuggler of historic artifacts and antiquities, Emrullah Gungor, was implicated in a major uranium smuggling case in Istanbul in 1994. Adolf Jaekle was arrested in Germany that same year, in possession of a small amount of high-grade plutonium. Jaekle had previously smuggled cigarettes and counterfeit currency.

After 1991, Russia became the center of organized crime in the world, with criminals gaining significant influence in the Russian army and police departments. Russia's Ministry of Internal Affairs International Crime Department reported in 1997 that more than 100 Russian criminal groups conducted illegal activities in foreign states. The Russian mafias are active in financial operations, drug trafficking, and illegal conventional weapons sales. They have close ties with Italian, Colombian, and Arab criminal groups.

Organized crime is increasingly becoming politicized in nations around the world because criminal goals can be furthered whenever politicians and political parties are controlled.

NATIONS COVERTLY PRODUCING WMD

With more than twenty nations known to have the ability and interest to produce WMD, it is difficult to know exactly who is producing them outside the bounds of international law.

In 1996, the World Court stated that using atomic weapons would violate the laws of war and that nations have a binding obligation to abolish them. But the number of nations with atomic weapons has grown since then. Nations that have covertly sponsored atomic weapons programs include India, Iran, Iraq, Israel, North Korea, Libya, Pakistan, and possibly Syria. There are also five formally declared nuclear powers—China, France, Russia, Great Britain, and the United States.

INDIA

There is a great deal of terrorism in India, with at least 20,000 people, including prime ministers and national leaders, killed in the province of Kashmir since 1990. Terrorism in India is typically motivated by ethnic and religious concerns.

India detonated an underground atomic bomb in May 1998, marking the success of its covert weapons program. India obtained assistance for its atomic power plants in 2000, primarily from Russia and western Europe. With new foreign equipment, India could produce more sophisticated atomic weapons.

India tested three short-range missiles between January and June 2000. India has also stockpiled enough plutonium to make an estimated sixty to eighty atomic weapons, according to Leonard Spector, who tracked nuclear proliferation for the Carnegie Endowment for International Peace.

An Indian soldier stands at attention by a Prithvi missile during a holiday parade in New Delhi, India. The Prithvi missile is capable of carrying a nuclear warhead.

IRAN

Terrorist operations under Ayatollah Khomeini made Iran the chief sponsor of international terrorism in the 1980s. Iran has suffered economically because the United States and other countries imposed sanctions that prohibit foreign trade and financial aid.

To choke off Iran's supply of materials and technology, the United States also applied sanctions against chemical and equipment companies in Europe. Iran turned to Russia, China, Pakistan, and North Korea, which were responsive to its needs. In August 2002, an exiled Iranian opposition group revealed that Iran was secretly building atomic facilities.

Iran is also capable of producing many different kinds of biological weapons. Iran has manufactured blister, blood, choking, and nerve agents, along with the artillery shells to deliver them. Iran has one of the largest missile inventories in the Middle East and is producing more long-range versions.

In December 2003, worldwide pressure forced Iran to allow the United Nations to conduct nuclear inspections inside the country on short notice. Iran declared it would suspend uranium production and provide full details of its atomic programs dating back to the 1980s. Iran's pledge is a major step toward world peace.

IRAQ

After the Gulf War in 1991, many biological and chemical weapons were discovered in Iraq. The Iraqis admitted that they had produced enormous quantities of chemical weapons: 2,850 tons of mustard gas, 790 tons of sarin, and 290 tons of tabun. The Iraqi government of former dictator Saddam Hussein used chemical attacks in 1987 on the Kurds and Shiites, dissident members of the population.

Iraq had also produced biological weapons: 1,717 gallons (6,500 L) of anthrax and 2,642 gallons (10,000 L) of botulinum. Botulinum is the most deadly toxin available. It is 100,000 times more poisonous than sarin gas. Theoretically, 18 pounds (8.2 kg) of botulinum is enough, in optimum weather conditions, to kill everyone within 60 square miles (155.4 sq. km) of the dispersal site.

At one time, the Iraqi atomic program employed 15,000 people. These employees worked at more than twenty sites, costing $10 billion over a decade prior to the Iraqi invasion of Kuwait. Yet despite this large-scale program, no atomic weapons were found in Iraq after Saddam Hussein was removed from power in 2003, during the United States–led Operation Iraqi Freedom. The Carnegie Endowment for International Peace stated in January 2004 that Bush administration officials had "systematically misrepresented the threat from Iraq's WMD and ballistic missile programs." The endowment outlined its charge in a report entitled "WMD in Iraq: Evidence and Implications."

ISRAEL

Israel is believed to possess 100 nuclear warheads, but it refuses to confirm or deny its status. The Israeli nuclear weapons program reportedly started in the 1950s. As early as 1949, Israel performed a geological survey of the Negev Desert, looking for natural uranium reserves.

It is believed that Israel had two atomic bombs in 1967 that were readied for use during the Six-Day War, and more weapons that were prepped during the Yom Kippur War of 1973.

In 1986, nuclear technician Mordechai Vanunu gave a London newspaper photographs and information about the Dimona nuclear weapons facility where he had worked. Vanunu was tried for treason and sentenced to prison for eighteen years. He was released in April 2004. In late 2001, other former employees claimed that the aging Dimona reactor is in danger of a meltdown and that workers are at risk of radiation poisoning.

NORTH KOREA

North Korea followed Iran's lead in January 2004, offering to freeze its atomic weapons and energy programs. In exchange, North Korea requested economic aid and security guarantees. The United States asked that North Korea begin dismantling its nuclear weapons programs before any concessions were given.

This offer came six months after North Korea openly threatened to build enough atomic weapons to deter other countries from attacking it.

Mordechai Vanunu displays a copy of the newspaper article for which he had provided information on Israel's secret nuclear weapons program. After his release from prison, Vanunu declared that he did not regret exposing Israel's nuclear capabilities.

In April 2003, North Korea announced that it possessed atomic weapons and intended to create more. North Korea also manufactures long-range missiles capable of reaching the United States.

North Korea has stockpiled chemical weapons and has the ability to produce bulk quantities of nerve, blister, choking, and blood agents using its chemical industry. The country has also created biological weapons since the 1960s.

LIBYA

In another recent development, Libyan leader Muʻammar Gadhafi pledged in December 2003 to give up efforts to develop an atomic weapon. When inspectors went into Libya, they found centrifuges and other equipment for producing atomic weapons. The head of the

UN watchdog agency stated the country was at an early stage of its nuclear weapons program. The Libyans began developing atomic technology in the 1970s.

Gadhafi has ruled Libya for more than three decades. Throughout his rule, Libya supported a number of terrorist groups. Libya was implicated in the 1988 bombing of Pan Am Flight 103 over Lockerbie, Scotland.

Economic sanctions, which prohibited businesses from trading in Libya, produced results. As Prime Minister Shokri Ghanem of Libya stated, "We can't afford guns and butter." A small country of 5 million people, Libya intends to attract investment and trade in exchange for its rich reserves of oil. Libya has also made overtures to end its chemical and biological weapons programs.

SYRIA

Syria is one of several states in the Middle East developing chemical and biological weapons. Syria's efforts began in 1973 with the transfer of chemical weapons equipment and supplies from Egypt.

According to U.S. intelligence agencies, Syria currently has a significant stockpile of sarin and is trying to develop the more deadly VX chemical gas. Syria produces several tons of chemicals every year. It also has missiles capable of carrying chemical warheads, which were tested in 1999.

Syria continues to develop biological weapons. However, it still requires extensive foreign assistance to reach its goals. This is also true of its atomic program, which Syria denies exists. Though it has a nuclear research center at Dayr al Hajar, Syria would have to rely on foreign assistance for materials, equipment, and experts in order to achieve its objective.

PAKISTAN

Pakistan announced that it had successfully conducted six atomic tests in May 1998, just two weeks after its longtime rival India tested its atomic weapons. Pakistan claimed that the explosions created an earthquake that was 5.0 on the Richter scale.

Pakistani protesters demonstrate in support of Abdul Qadeer Khan, the father of Pakistan's nuclear program. In January 2004, Khan confessed to illegally providing nuclear technology to Iran, North Korea, and Libya.

Pakistan created a clandestine network to obtain materials and technology to enrich uranium, working directly with China and acquiring dual-use equipment and materials from former Soviet states and western Europe. Since 1975, Pakistan's atomic weapons program has been run by Dr. Abdul Qadeer Khan. Dr. Khan is a German-trained metallurgist with extensive knowledge that he acquired at the classified URENCO uranium enrichment plant in the Netherlands. Dr. Khan also reportedly provided Pakistan with stolen uranium enrichment technologies from Europe.

In January 2004, Khan confessed to illegally transferring nuclear technology to Iran, Libya, and North Korea. He was sentenced to house arrest, but was quickly pardoned by Pakistani president Pervez Musharraf.

WEAPONS OF MASS DESTRUCTION: ILLICIT TRADE AND TRAFFICKING

The Carnegie Endowment for International Peace reports that Pakistan has produced between 1,290 and 1,764 pounds (585 and 800 kg) of highly enriched uranium, enough for 30 to 55 atomic weapons. Pakistan is also believed to have biological weapons development programs, yet it officially denies it. ■

> The Russian government, with substantial contributions from France, Norway, Sweden, and the United Kingdom, has spent considerable funds to rehabilitate this nuclear waste depository in the Andreyeva Guba, Russia. The site now ranks among the safest in the former Soviet states.

4 WHAT ARE THE AUTHORITIES DOING ABOUT IT?

With the exception of Libya's remarkable disarmament, the eight nations discussed in the previous chapter appear to have little motivation for giving up their WMD development programs. The same goes for the numerous other countries with chemical and biological weapons, as well as the five formally declared nuclear

WEAPONS OF MASS DESTRUCTION:
ILLICIT TRADE AND TRAFFICKING

powers. Many of these nations believe their only protection from invasion is their weapons programs. Therefore, it is up to the governments of the world to protect their citizens by prohibiting the trade and trafficking of dangerous materials.

Yet even the United States, which has the best export system in the world, can't control every dual-use material or technology. Control merely buys time for other methods to work, such as sanctions against businesses and nations.

One ongoing effort has provided hundreds of millions of dollars for Russian projects funded through the International Science and Technology Center (ISTC). The ISTC provides peaceful civilian employment opportunities for scientists and engineers of the former Soviet Union involved with WMD and their delivery systems. It is funded by the United States, the European Union, Norway, Japan, and Canada.

Diplomatic pressure, along with recent military campaigns in the Middle East, has also been successful in deterring some nations from protecting terrorists or sponsoring terrorism. Nations are strongly encouraged to join the international agreements that deal with the trade and smuggling of dangerous materials.

Since 1957, the International Atomic Energy Agency's member states have taken responsibility for combating illicit trade and trafficking of atomic material within their own borders. The IAEA started with 81 nations and has grown to include 137 as of October 2003. Many of these member states have called for greater international efforts to counter illicit trade of atomic material.

AGREEMENTS, REGULATIONS, AND TREATIES

For decades, there have been numerous treaties, agreements, laws, and other efforts to prevent the trade and trafficking of dangerous materials. The United States and Russia renounced the use or possession of biological weapons in 1972, at the Biological Weapons Convention. Yet both countries maintain "defensive" research facilities that employ dangerous biological materials in making antidotes.

WHAT ARE THE AUTHORITIES DOING ABOUT IT?

WHY INSPECTIONS DON'T ALWAYS WORK

Inspection teams from the International Atomic Energy Agency (IAEA) visited Libya regularly until December 2003, when that country agreed to cease its weapons programs. But the inspectors were shocked when they went into Libya a week later and found equipment that could be used to make atomic bombs, some of it piled in dirt alleyways.

In a December 30, 2003, article, *Washington Post* reporter Daniel Williams quotes the director of the IAEA, Mohamed ElBaradei, as having admitted, "Low-level programs like this are difficult to detect. They can be run in a garage. You would have to be lucky or have very good intelligence to run across it. We're doing a lot of soul-searching."

The discovery in Libya highlights the problem with relying on international inspections to stop weapons programs. The IAEA director appealed to countries to use diplomatic means to resolve disputes and reduce the temptation for governments to acquire weapons of mass destruction, especially in the Middle East.

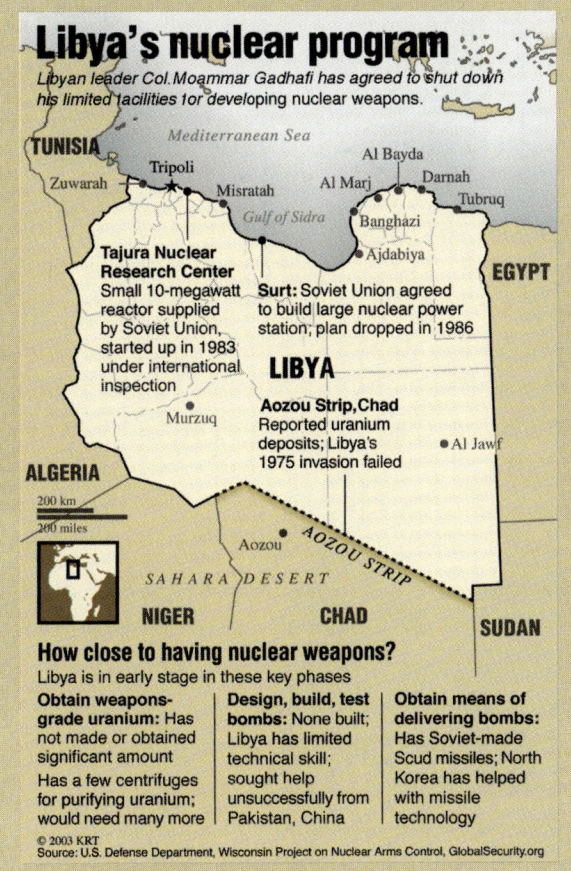

This illustration, published in December 2003, details what was known about the sources and extent of Libya's nuclear weapons program at the time.

In order to protect the legal material that is readily available, the Export Administration Act of 1979 prohibited companies or individuals from knowingly exporting any materials or technologies that would assist a foreign government or terrorist group in developing WMD.

The United States became a member of the Australia Group in the mid-1980s. This informal association of thirty-four nations monitors the trade of materials that can be developed into WMD. The member nations are attempting to coordinate their laws controlling this material, and are developing guidelines for detecting when material is being transported.

Unfortunately, the number of nations that have joined limits the effectiveness of the Australia Group. Most of the member nations are European, and there is little or no participation from other parts of the world, including Africa and South America.

Within the United States, terrorists are prohibited from acquiring biological weapons under the Biological Weapons Anti-Terrorism Act of 1989. Congress then passed the Chemical and Biological Weapons Control Act of 1991. This legislation called for economic and diplomatic sanctions, such as canceling humanitarian aid for countries that use biological weapons against international law. Sanctions may also be imposed on any foreign company that knowingly exports materials to prohibited countries such as Iran and North Korea.

After the fall of the Soviet Union in 1991, the United States created cooperative programs with Russia that were supported by U.S. funds and expertise. These efforts helped upgrade the physical security at weapon sites, improved accounting procedures, and worked toward protecting the transport of nuclear warheads to dismantling and storage sites. The United States has spent $5 billion since the end of the Cold War to help Russia safeguard its nuclear materials and weapons.

In 1993, both the United States and Russia signed the Chemical Weapons Convention treaty, which prohibits the use, production, stockpiling, trade, and acquisition of chemical weapons. In 1997, both countries ratified this treaty. However, neither the United States nor Russia will be able to destroy its large stockpiles of chemical weapons before 2007, at the very least.

A Ukrainian worker dismantles the booster of a SS-19 nuclear missile at the missile dismantling site in Dnepropetrovsk, Ukraine, on February, 26, 1999. Within five years of the collapse of the Soviet Union, the Ukraine transferred all of its nuclear weapons to Russia in exchange for fuel for its nuclear power plant.

The Centers for Disease Control and Prevention was instructed to maintain a list of biological agents that "pose a severe threat to public health and safety." The current list includes more than thirty viruses, bacteria, and toxins. Any trade of these restricted materials must be registered with the federal and state governments.

For atomic weapons, the current treaties are merely guidelines for the nuclear nations. Under the 1993 START II Treaty, the United States and Russia were supposed to reduce their nuclear warheads to 3,500 each. The United States formally withdrew from the Treaty on Limitation of Anti-Ballistic Missile Systems (ABM Treaty) in order to develop a prohibited missile defense system. Russia responded by withdrawing from START II in June 2002. Currently, both countries are

Mohamed ElBaradei, director general of the International Atomic Energy Agency, discusses Iran and Libya's violation of the Non-Proliferation Treaty with members of the press on March 8, 2004, in Vienna, Austria. In addition to its role in controlling the proliferation of nuclear weapons, The IAEA helps develop peaceful applications of nuclear technology.

operating under the SORT Treaty of 2002, which calls for the storage of nuclear warheads rather than their dismantling.

TRACKING DANGEROUS MATERIALS

Biological and chemical weapons are nearly impossible to track. Almost any country with chemical and pharmaceutical industries can produce weapons. Chemicals and biological samples can be mislabeled and transported as legal material.

Uranium and plutonium are much easier to track because there are a limited number of governments with the ability to produce enriched atomic material. The IAEA's Radiological Security Partnership attempts to prevent the development of atomic weapons by keeping track of atomic materials. The United States contributed $3 million to support this effort in 2003.

Currently, sixty-nine countries have agreed to report incidents of illicit trafficking to the IAEA. As of January 2002, over 400 incidents of nuclear trafficking (of both weapons-grade and non-weapons-grade materials) had been reported to the IAEA, with sixty-three incidents in 2001 alone. The IAEA stressed that the total number of attempts is likely much higher.

Most smuggling cases involve small amounts of atomic material that are of little value in making a weapon. Interpol and other law enforcement agencies track even minor amounts including plutonium screws, single plutonium tablets, and smoke alarms containing plutonium. This is necessary because enough atomic material could be gathered together to make a dirty bomb.

There is also concern because even small amounts of atomic material can inflict fatal radiation on the smugglers and anyone around them. The IAEA considers smuggling to be a serious issue of public health.

It may be reassuring to know that the black market is filled with scam artists. According to the German Federal Criminal Police, in as many as 25 to 50 percent of the offers for atomic materials, the sellers fail to deliver. Quoted prices are also extremely high, sometimes hundreds of times higher than legitimate selling prices, which discourage prospective customers from buying.

CONCLUSION

Experts have concluded that the problems of illicit trade and trafficking should be dealt with by preventing the exchange of dangerous materials. The best preventive measures are controlling the borders, enforcing strict export licensing, and securing sites that hold dangerous materials. Each country must voluntarily agree to enforce international agreements and have the funds to police their own populations in order to prevent illicit trade and trafficking.

Though change is coming slowly, the good news is that countries such as Libya have taken steps to renounce their WMD programs. They are opening their doors to allow international inspectors into their countries. Since 1989, a dozen other nations have renounced their intentions of

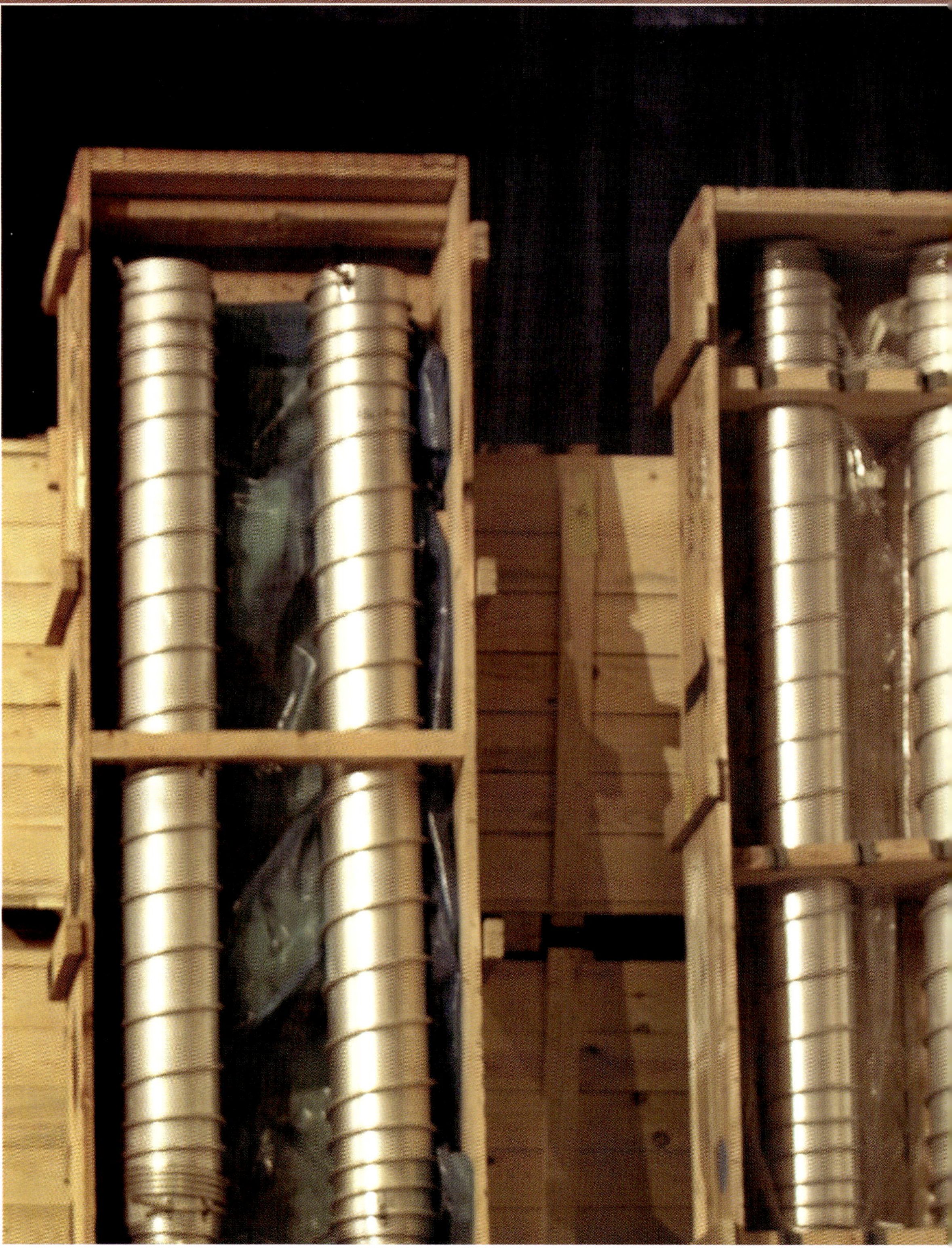

The components of Libya's nuclear weapons program were shipped to the United States in January 2004, after Libya decided to become a nuclear-free state. They are housed at the Y-12 National Security Complex in Oak Ridge, Tennessee, under heavy security.

maintaining atomic weapons or have dismantled their weapons programs. There is a general optimism that stockpiles of weapons of mass destruction will continue to be reduced and stored safely out of the reach of terrorists and rogue nations.

[GLOSSARY]

agent A substance capable of producing a chemical reaction or a physical effect on people, animals, or plants.

black market The covert network for trading illegal goods that is not governed by regulatory measures.

Cold War The political tension and weapons buildup that existed between the United States and the Soviet Union following World War II. The Cold War ended in 1991 with the fall of the Soviet Union.

conventional weapons Traditional weapons such as guns and bombs that do not include atomic material or chemical and biological agents.

dirty bomb A bomb made of explosives and a small amount of atomic material.

dual-use materials Materials used to make atomic, chemical or biological weapons that have legitimate uses in research, energy production, medical applications, and industries.

export license A license granted by a country allowing a company or individual to transport and trade specific materials.

IAEA International Atomic Energy Agency; an agency that polices illegal development of nuclear weapons programs and works with nations around the world to promote safe, secure, and peaceful nuclear technologies

ICBM Intercontinental ballistic missile; a missile that is capable of traveling from one continent to another.

Interpol International Criminal Police Organization; the international law enforcement agency.

nuclear Energy that is generated from atomic matter.

nuclear warheads Atomic bombs carried by missiles.

rogue nation A country that is covertly developing weapons of mass destruction in violation of international agreements, or sponsors terrorism.

sanction A penalty imposed by a country against a business or nation that violates international law.

weapons-grade Relating to atomic, chemical, or biological material that is pure enough to make a weapon.

weapons of mass destruction (WMD) Atomic, chemical, and biological weapons that are capable of inflicting large numbers of casualties and widespread property damage.

FOR MORE INFORMATION

Carnegie Endowment for International Peace
1779 Massachusetts Avenue NW
Washington, DC 20036-2103
(202) 483-7600
Web site: http://www.ceip.org

Center for International Trade and Security
120 Holmes/Hunter Academic Building, University of Georgia
Athens, GA 30602
(706) 542-2985
Web site: http://www.uga.edu/cits/home/index.htm

The Centers for Disease Control and Prevention
1600 Clifton Road
Atlanta, GA 30333
(800) 311-3435
Web site: http://www.cdc.gov

International Atomic Energy Agency (IAEA)
P.O. Box 100
Wagramer Strasse 5, A-1400
Vienna, Austria
Web site: http://www.iaea.org/

International Criminal Police Organization (Interpol)
General Secretariat
200, quai Charles de Gaulle
69006 Lyon, France
Web site: http://www.interpol.int/Public/Icpo/default.asp

The U.S. Nuclear Regulatory Commission
Office of Public Affairs
Washington, DC 20055
(800) 368-5642
Web site: http://www.nrc.gov

Terrorism Questions and Answers by the Council on
Foreign Relations
1779 Massachusetts Avenue NW
Washington, DC 20036
(202) 518-3400
Web site: http://www.terrorismanswers.com/home

WEB SITES

Due to the changing nature of Internet links, the Rosen Publishing Group, Inc., has developed an online list of Web sites related to the subject of this book. This site is updated regularly. Please use this link to access the list:

http://www.rosenlinks.com/lwmd/wmditt

FOR FURTHER READING

Bertsch, Gary K., and William C. Potter, eds. *Dangerous Weapons, Desperate States: Russia, Belarus, Kazakstan, and Ukraine.* New York: Routledge, 1999.

Laqueur, Walter. *The New Terrorism: Fanaticism and the Arms of Mass Destruction.* New York: Oxford University Press, 1999.

Lee, Rensselaer W., III. *Smuggling Armageddon: The Nuclear Black Market in the Former Soviet Union and Europe.* New York: St. Martin's Press, 1998.

Schweitzer, Glenn E. *Super-Terrorism: Assassins, Mobsters, and Weapons of Mass Destruction.* New York: Plenum Trade, 1998.

Turner, Stansfield. *Caging the Genies: A Workable Solution for Nuclear, Chemical, and Biological Weapons.* Boulder, CO: Westview Press, 1999.

Williams, Paul, and Paul Woessner. "The Real Threat of Nuclear Smuggling," *Scientific American,* January 1996, pp. 40–44.

BIBLIOGRAPHY

Bertsch, Gary K. and Suzette R. Grillot, eds. *Arms on the Market: Reducing the Risk of Proliferation in the Former Soviet Union*. New York: Routledge, 1998.

Cilluffo, Frank J. "Combating Chemical, Biological, Radiological, and Nuclear Terrorism: A Comprehensive Strategy." A report of the CSIS Homeland Defense Project. Washington, DC: The CSIS Press, May 2001.

Cirincione, Joseph, ed. *Repairing the Regime: Preventing the Spread of Weapons of Mass Destruction*. New York: Routledge, 2000.

Cirincione, Joseph, Jessica T. Matthews, and George Perskovich. "WMD in Iraq: Evidence and Implications." Carnegie Endowment for International Peace. January 2004.

Dobbs, Michael. "Collapse of Soviet Union Proved Boon to Iranian Missile Program," *Washington Post*, January 13, 2002.

Dobbs, Michael. "A Story of Iran's Quest for Power; A Scientist Details the Role of Russia," *Washington Post*, January 13, 2002.

Ford, James L. "Nuclear Smuggling: How Serious a Threat?" *Strategic Forum Bulletin*. Washington, DC: Institute for National Strategic Studies, January 1996.

Gertz, Bill. "U.S. hits China with Sanctions over Arms Sales," *Washington Times*, January 25, 2002.

"Loose Nukes." Interview with Leonid Smirnov. PBS *Frontline*. November 20, 1997.

Nartker, Mike. "International Response I: Merge Export Control Regimes, Experts Say," Global Security Newswire, September 26, 2002.

Orlov, Vladimir. "Export Controls and Nuclear Smuggling in Russia," *Dangerous Weapons, Desperate States*. New York: Routledge, 1999.

Specter, Michael. "Occupation of a Nuclear Power Plant Signals Russian Labor's Anger," *New York Times*, December 7, 1996.

Spector, Leonard. *Nuclear Ambitions.* San Francisco: Westview Press, 1990.

Williams, Daniel. "Nuclear Program in Libya Detailed: Research at Early Stage, U.N. Inspectors Report," *Washington Post*, December 30, 2003.

INDEX

A

Al Qaeda, 30, 35
anthrax, 22, 35, 39
atomic engineers, 4, 5, 6, 17
atomic material, theft/smuggling of, 22, 23, 33, 35
atomic weapons
   about, 9–10, 12
   dual-use materials and, 19
   inspections and, 47
   making, 14, 16, 19, 22
   nations with, 37, 39–44, 47
   tracking, 50–51
   treaties on, 49–50
Aum Shinrikyo, 15, 17
Australia Group, 48

B

bin Laden, Osama, 35
biological weapons
   about, 12–14
   Al Qaeda and, 35
   dual-use materials and, 19
   laws and, 48, 49
   making, 15–16, 17, 19, 22
   nations with, 39, 41, 42, 44, 45
   tracking, 50
Biological Weapons Convention, 46
black market, 6–7, 26-28, 51
botulinum, 39

C

Carnegie Endowment for International Peace, 37, 40, 44
Centers for Disease Control and Prevention, 49

cesium 137, 10, 22, 25
Chechnya/Chechens, 10, 29
chemical weapons
   about, 10–11, 12, 13
   Al Qaeda and, 35
   dual-use materials and, 19
   making, 16, 17
   nations with, 39, 41, 42, 45
   tracking, 50
   treaties/laws on, 48
Chemical Weapons Convention, 48
China, 13-14, 18, 24, 26, 37, 39, 43
   exportation of weapons-grade material, 24, 26
cobalt 60, 10, 22
Cold War, 9, 14, 48
customs agencies, 29–31, 51

D

dirty bomb, 10, 35, 51
disgruntled employees, 4, 6
dual-use materials, 19–22, 24, 43, 36

E

ElBaradei, Mohamed, 47

G

Gadhafi, Mu'ammar, 41, 42
Great Britain, 37

F

France, 37

G

germ warfare, 12
Gungor, Emrullah, 36

62

INDEX

H
Hussein, Saddam, 39, 40

I
India, 26, 37, 42
inspections, weapons, 39, 47, 51
International Atomic Energy Agency (IAEA), 28, 46, 47, 50–51
International Criminal Police Organization (Interpol), 28, 51
International Science and Technology Center, 46
Internet, information available on, 11, 14, 16
Iran, 17, 18, 26, 37, 39, 40, 43, 48
Iraq, 9, 10, 37, 39–40
Israel, 37, 40

J
Jaekle, Adolf, 36
Japan, 13–14, 17, 46
    sarin attack in, 15

K
Khan, Abdul Qadeer, 43–44

L
Lebed, Aleksandr, 25
Libya, 10, 18, 26, 37, 41–42, 43, 47
    disarmament of, 41–42, 45, 47, 51

M
Musharraf, Pervez, 43

N
North Korea, 26, 37, 39, 40–41, 43, 48

O
organized crime, 36–37
Orlov, Vladimir, 29

P
Pakistan, 26, 37, 39, 42–44
plague, 13

R
ricin, 22, 35
rogue nations, 9, 21, 54
Russia/Soviet Union
    exportation of weapons-grade material, 24, 25–26, 39, 43
    organized crime in, 36-37
    theft/smuggling of weapons-grade materials and, 4–6, 9, 10, 14, 23, 25, 28-29, 30, 32–33, 35
    treaties and, 48, 49–50
    weapons of mass destruction and, 9, 11, 22–23, 25

S
sarin, 15, 39, 42
September 11, 2001, terrorist attacks, 9, 29, 35
Smirnov, Leonid, 4–5, 7, 18
smuggling, 7, 10, 24, 26–29, 30, 32, 33, 35, 51
START II, 50
Syria, 37, 42

T
terrorists
    Al Qaeda, 30, 35
    atomic bombs and, 10, 14, 17
    biological weapons and, 17
    chemical weapons and, 10, 17
    dirty bombs and, 10
    getting materials to make WMD, 21, 33–35
    in India, 37
    in Iran, 39
    in Libya, 42
    providing protection/assistance to, 46, 48

reasons for wanting WMD, 7
  in the United States,
    8-9, 11
Tikhomirov, Alexei, 33
Treaty on Strategic Offensive
  Reductions, 22

U
United Nations, 39, 42
U.S. Customs Service, 30-31

V
Vanunu, Mordechai, 40
Vorobei, Vadim, 17-18

W
weapons of mass destruction
  attacks with, 15, 35
  concerns about, 8-9
  efforts to prevent trade/trafficking of,
    46-48
  knowledge needed to make, 16-17, 22
  nations with ability to produce, 37-44
  technology needed to make, 14-16
  theft from labs, 4, 7, 22, 24
  tracking, 50-51

Y
Yablokov, Alexei, 25

ABOUT THE AUTHOR
Susan Wright is a freelance writer living in New York City. She has written books and interactive workbooks on science and popular culture.

CREDITS
Cover, pp. 4–5 © TASS/Sovfoto; p. 6 WGBH-TVBoston/Media Library and Archives; p. 8 © AFP/Getty Images; p. 11 © Hulton/Archive/Getty Images; pp. 12–13, 14, 16–17, 27 (right), 41, 43 © AP/Wide World Photos; p. 15 Kyodo; p. 19 © East News/Getty Images; pp. 20–21 U.S. Department of Energy/Science Photo Library; p. 23 Thomas Nilsen/Science Photo Library; p. 25 © le Segretain Pascal/Corbis Sygma; p. 27 (left) Yuri Belinsky/ITAR-TASS/Newscom; pp. 28, 47 KRT/Newscom; p. 30 Roger L. Wollenberg/UPI/Landov; p. 32 Valentin Kuzmin/ITAR-TASS/Newscom; p. 34 © John Li/Getty Images; pp. 36, 50 © EPA/AP/Wide World Photos; p. 38 © Emmanuel Dunand/AFP/Getty Images; p. 45 © Lev Fedoseyev/ITAR-TASS/Newscom; p. 49 © Reuters/Corbis; pp. 52–53 © Paul Efird/Knoxville News Sentinel/Reuters/Corbis.

Designer: Evelyn Horovicz; Editor: Wayne Anderson;
Photo Researcher: Amy Feinberg

HOMESTEAD H.S. MEDIA CENTER
4310 HOMESTEAD ROAD
FORT WAYNE, IN 46814